STEAM MEMORIES 1950

No.31: Around NOTTINGHAM and its Environs

BOOK LAW PUBLICATIONS

Introduction.

John Cowlishaw was a Nottingham lad who in 1954, at the age of fifteen, started to take a serious interest in railway photography. Coupled with the fact that his father worked for British Railways in the city (exLMS side) and that John had a travelling streak, he was able to use either passes or privilege tickets to travel the country by train.

In this album however, John concentrates on the local railway network bordering Nottingham and those lines within the boundaries of the city to present us with a miscellany of views from Trowell on the Erewash valley main line, Bulwell to the north, Attenborough in the south and Rolleston junction to the east. We visit Colwick and Nottingham Midland engine sheds, besides the two main stations - Midland and Victoria.

One particular event in 1955 is highlighted and will no doubt arouse memories for the football fans amongst you, especially the Notts. County supporters. Anyway enjoy what is on offer because much of the infrastructure and virtually everything with wheels is now long gone.

John's interest in railways waned somewhat in 1959 when military affairs took up most of his spare time so to supplement the decade starting in 1960 we have included a number of photographs taken by another local railway photographer, the late Don Beecroft, who managed by a complete stroke luck or was it inside knowledge, to be at Daybrook on the last day of through running on the 'Back line'.

(title page) **Bagthorpe junction, September 1960. V2 No.60877 (honest) works north with a Bournemouth-Newcastle express. D.H.Beecroft.**

Printed and bound by The Amadeus Press, Cleckheaton, West Yorkshire.
First published in the United Kingdom by Book Law Publications, 382 Carlton Hill, Nottingham, NG4 1JA

The next station up from Trent, on the Midland line from Derby to Nottingham was Attenborough and on Christmas Eve 1955 LMS 4P Compound No.40929 slows with a stopping service from Nottingham to Derby. The 4-4-0 was one of the Vulcan Foundry built examples from 1927 and by now their days as first choice motive power for express passenger services were long gone. Withdrawals of the 195 strong class had started in 1952 and by the end of 1955 nearly half of them had been scrapped. It was No.40929's turn for the axe in July of the following year, the venue - Derby works. Note the somewhat lightweight character of the buildings and the narrow platforms of Attenborough station; all very nice for a quiet station but this place had two periods of extreme use, firstly in World War One when the National Shell Filling factory at Chilwell was opened to cope with the demands of the big guns of the Western Front. By the end of that conflict some 10,000 people worked at the site and the station was handling three times its normal annual number of passengers. After a period of quiet the factory at Chilwell was once again called upon to supply armaments for WW2 and the station came into its own again. Up to the early sixties' there used to be a regular working from Ollerton which travelled via Lenton South junction and terminated here. The first Midland station on this site, known as Attenborough Gate, was opened in December 1856 but closed in November 1858. In September 1864 it was re-opened without the Gate suffix. The place is still open today.

Passing the maltings of the local brewery, Fairburn Class 4P No.42174 works a Derby-Nottingham 'stopper' into Beeston station on Christmas Eve 1955. When Derby works turned out this 2-6-4T new in October 1948 it was designated to be allocated to Carstairs shed but Derby shed kept it 'on loan' until April 1949 when it was eventually released to the Scottish depot. However, it was back at Derby in December 1950 and stayed at 17A until September 1962 except for a one month loan to Trafford Park in December 1958. Leicester got it from Derby and in April 1963 it moved further south to Bedford. The following August it came back north but this time to Stockport Edgeley shed who kept it for just five months until its final depot, Wigan's Springs Branch, beckoned. Withdrawal came in August 1965 and it was sold to Cashmores yard at Newport in Monmouthshire later in the year.

LMS Class 4F 0-6-0 No.44161 passes through Beeston station and under the west end footbridge on Saturday 24th December 1955, with a westbound goods train. The original Beeston station was opened on 4th June 1839 by the Midland Counties Railway and is still in use today albeit in a rebuilt form, however, the date plate on the wall above the canopy of the main station building reveals a date of 1842! Was this the finishing date of a partially opened station which had been hurriedly put into use for the opening of the line from Nottingham to Derby? The 4F was built at Crewe in 1926 as part of the LMS (Midlandisation) locomotive standardisation policy and was any early candidate for withdrawal, being amongst the first forty-four of the class condemned in 1959. It had certainly been around the old LMS Midland Division during its life, being stationed at various periods to Skipton, Royston, Toton and Nottingham, amongst others. On this date in 1955 it was a Roton engine and remained until condemned.

At the other end of the station on the same afternoon, an empty mineral train bound for one of the Leen Valley collieries, rumbles through behind clanking WD 2-8-0 No.90369. The 2-8-0 was based at Northampton shed at this time and was one of four sent there in March 1954 for workings such as these to the Nottinghamshire pits. All four engines left together in April 1957, two going to Birkenhead and the other pair to Mold Junction shed. Note the nice curving cast iron footbridge at this end which obviously dates from a different period to the rather austere structure at the western end of the platforms. And, how about the ornate roof boards on the station building - it seems there was no expense spared during certain periods of railway building and expansion.

This view from the footbridge at the east end of Beeston station on 24th December 1955, reveals plenty of activity in the extensive goods facility on the north side of the line, behind the signal box. Just beyond the livestock platform there appears to be a grounded clerestory carriage in use as one of the yard huts or offices. The advertisement hoarding, overlooking the Meadow Road level crossing gates, features a well known (at the time) margarine trying to push itself as the post-war alternative to a wartime rationed natural substance which was then becoming more plentiful. Oh, the footbridge was also a great place to watch or photograph trains from. Nottingham allocated Johnson 2P No.40411 is showing express headlamps but what the service was I do not know.

The tonnage of coal which has trundled through the Midland's Erewash valley on the main line to Toton marshalling yard must equate to more than a billion tons during the age of steam alone. The flow from the Derbyshire and Nottinghamshire collieries was phenomenal to say the least and, industrial action apart, it was a six day a week operation for the railway with staging and concentration yards from Chesterfield to Stanton Gate. Engine sheds also marked the route, Hasland, Westhouses, Toton and of course those not quite on the valley route but which fed onto the main line with their local colliery production. Ex MR Fowler 4F No.43845, itself a Toton resident, epitomised the long time motive power on this route, the 0-6-0 tender engine. Here at Trowell, on a summer evening in 1957, the forty-odd year old locomotive is drifting down to Toton with a heavy train of industrial coal.

Another coal movement through Trowell towards Toton on the same evening. Such was the nature of the traffic - it just kept coming. Stanier 8F 2-8-0 No.48541 represents the next development of LMS heavy haulage motive power and these engines certainly became popular with the LMS and the War Department who between them had more than eight hundred and fifty of these superb locomotives. BR eventually had six hundred and sixty-six Stanier 8F's in stock and during the last year of steam operations on BR nearly two hundred were active. 48541 was one of the LNER built examples and was turned out from Darlington in January 1944 ready to work in the north-east, first at Heaton shed then from Tyne Dock shed in September 1946. It came to the LMS in November 1946, being allocated to Grimesthorpe shed. Stints at Cricklewood, Mansfield and finally Kirkby-in-Ashfield brought it to its June 1966 withdrawal, just twenty-two years old. Note the superb condition of this main line which was not a race track for crack expresses but a main artery for the humble coal train, hundreds of them every week.

This section of the Erewash valley main line could boast six running tracks - it needed them, note the train on the far right. Hammering through Trowell with coke empties in 1957, are two Stanier 8F's headed by No.48138 carrying express freight lamps. Empty mineral wagons got as much priority, if not more, as loaded mineral wagons because the pits could not discharge the coal without the empty wagons. So, it became a continuous cycle of wagons or perhaps more like a vicious circle. Customers were the biggest problem as they would receive a loaded wagon of coal and keep hold of the wagon until the coal was either required or unloaded. Therefore, in extreme cases wagons could be tied up for weeks but generally it was a matter of about a week. Add the time a wagon spent out on the line with the time in yards and it is easy to realise why so many coal wagons were needed to keep the supplies moving. No wonder the MGR system was so successful in getting rid of hundreds of thousands of mineral wagons. No.48138 was one of the Crewe built 8F's and was allocated to Holbeck shed when new in 1941. Its next move was to Kirkby-in-Ashfield in February 1948 where it resided until June 1954 except for a one month loan to Stourton in September 1948. Saltley had it for five months in 1954 before it went to Canklow. It was transferred to the former Great Northern shed at Ardsley in September 1959 and then Wakefield during the following June. Its stay at 56A was brief because it moved finally to Mirfield in November 1960. Withdrawn in October 1965, it was purchased by T.W.Ward who cut it up in their yard at Killamarsh in March 1966. The station here, note it only served the two middle tracks, was opened in June 1884 and closed 2nd January 1967.

Trains heading north from Nottingham used to gain the Erewash valley main line by way of a route which took them through Lenton, Radford, Wollaton and then Trowell to join the main line just south of Trowell station, following the course of the Nottingham canal for much of the way. This cut-through saved a number of miles and kept the trains clear of the busy junctions around Trent and Toton. Coming around the curve towards Trowell at a fair old rate of knots on 3rd October 1955, is LMS 4P No.41198 and 'Jubilee' No.45659 DRAKE with a Leeds bound express. The compound was on its last legs, so to speak, and was withdrawn during the following December being broken up at Derby works before Christmas. Derby built No.45659 was one of only two 'Jubilees' which stayed at one shed throughout its working life. From new in December 1934 it was allocated to Leeds Holbeck and was withdrawn from there in May 1963. The other 'Jubilee' which had the same distinction was No.45658 KEYES, another Derby built engine which, ironically, was also allocated to Holbeck shed in December 1934 and outlived DRAKE by a couple of years, being withdrawn in September 1965.

Further up the line towards Nottingham on Thursday 10th November 1955, and accelerating away from Wollaton with a Down express, BR Standard No.73046 pilots Nottingham based 'Jubilee' No.45560 PRINCE EDWARD ISLAND. The Standard had been a Leicester Midland based engine since new in November 1953. In May 1958 it went to Millhouses and then on to Canklow in April 1961. In November 1962 it moved to the Southern Region, based at Nine Elms. During its nine years on the LMR it clocked up 337,580 miles. Withdrawal took place in September 64 when it was just over ten years old. The 'Jubilee' was one of the North British built members of the class and was delivered to Crewe North in July 1934. For the next three years it was sent to various Western Division sheds including Preston, Camden, Willesden, Carnforth before moving across to the Midland Division at Leeds Holbeck in August 1937. Nottingham acquired 45560 in September 1952 and kept it for five years before it returned westward to Edge Hill shed. Finally Crewe North got it back in June 1961. It was withdrawn in November 1963 and cut up at Crewe works.

Between Radford and Trowell is situated the district of Wollaton, now part of the growing Nottingham suburban sprawl and a place where communication has always been important. The Nottingham canal, A609 road and the former Midland Railway route between Nottingham and the Erewash valley all follow the same east-west course. The road was there first and it goes virtually dead-straight, any sudden change in grade being taken without hesitation. The canal builders had to follow the contours of the land but still had to put in numerous sets of locks to lift the navigation over the high land. The railway basically followed the course of the canal and on the way had to create some embankments, bridges and cuttings in order to keep the gradients as slight as possible. Around Wollaton railway cuttings became the order of the day and in April 1960 the Down WAVERLEY headed by 'Royal Scot' No.46100 ROYAL SCOT is accelerating westwards after negotiating the junction at Radford. This named train had one of the longest schedules of any in the country. Between St Pancras and Waverley it had by 1960 a dozen intermediate stations to stop at. This particular train would have left London at around 9-15 a.m. but would not arrive in Edinburgh until a few minutes before 7-0 p.m. with two engine changes en route. The Up train would fair no better leaving Waverley just after 10-0 a.m. with a St Pancras arrival of ten minutes to 8-0 p.m. However, it did have a restaurant car and the journey offered some superb countryside views, especially north of Leeds. Next stop Chesterfield. photograph - D.H.Beecroft.

Giltbrook viaduct on the Great Northern Railway's Derbyshire Extension was built during the years 1873 to 1875. The massive brick construction formed a somewhat straight letter 'S' in plan form. To accommodate local roads, railways and a branch of the Nottingham canal which were already established in the valley it spanned, certain of the arches were built on a skew. This view from the Awsworth Road of the eastern end of the viaduct in October 1956, highlights the first of the skewed arches. When the former Derbyshire Extension lines were closed in November 1964, this graceful viaduct was apparently listed for preservation but the motor car intervened and this great monument to Victorian engineering was demolished nine years later to make way for a by-pass. Rolling over the structure with an empty mineral train is Colwick J6 No.64269, itself with only three years life left before it too was broken up.

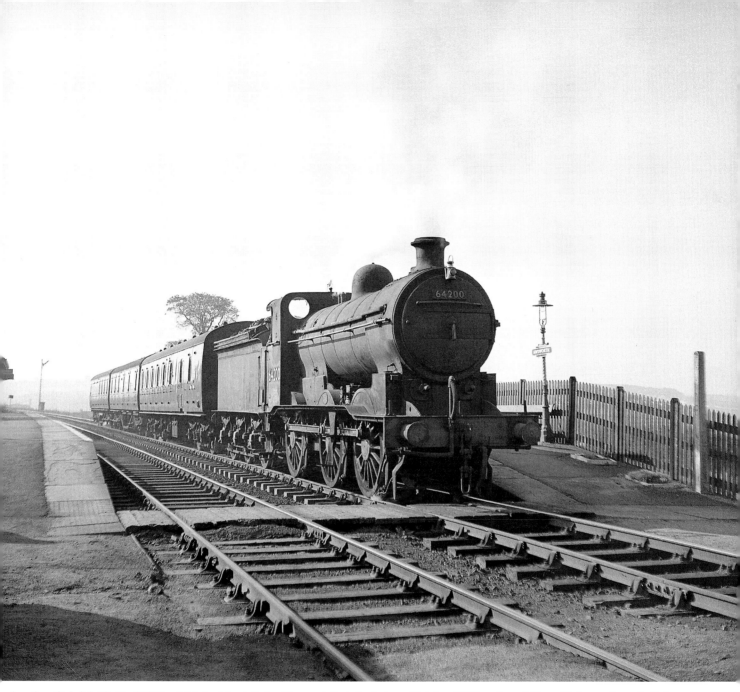

Another Colwick J6, No.64200, which incidentally had been at that shed since October 1927 and would be withdrawn there in February 1958, gets ready to draw away from Awsworth with an afternoon working from Derby (Friargate) to Nottingham (Victoria), 13th October 1956. This small station was opened in 1880 and closed with the rest of the Extension in September 1964.

About to depart from Awsworth with a train for Derby (Friargate) on 13th October 1956, Colwick A5 No.69821 works bunker first. Colwick employed nineteen of these GC designed 4-6-2 tank engines on these services during the 1950's, a couple would be outstationed at Derby shed to balance the light engine running. Note the cast iron gentlemen's urinal at the platform end - I wonder if it was a product of the nearby ironworks ? There is a similar preserved example at Crich Tramway village.

Getting a slight reprieve on the ten mile long (1 in 130) climb from Nottingham (Victoria) to Kirkby South junction on the ex GC main line, Low Moor based Stanier Cl.5 No.44912 heads THE SOUTH YORKSHIREMAN through the quarter mile of level road through Bulwell Common station on the evening of Wednesday 20th June 1956. On its way northward to Sheffield (Victoria), Huddersfield, Halifax and eventually Bradford (Exchange), this named train was a British Railways innovation and was introduced on 31st May 1948. Initially the ex LMS engine would work the Up train from Bradford, departing at approximately 10.00 a.m., to Sheffield (Victoria), where a Darnall B1 would take over and run the train as far as Leicester. Here, a Leicester based B1 would take the train into Marylebone for a 3.30 p.m. arrival. Normally the Low Moor Class 5 which came off the train at Sheffield, would then take a York-Bournemouth train south to Leicester and return with the northbound working of that train as far as Sheffield where it would await the Down, Bradford bound, working of THE SOUTH YORKSHIREMAN. At Sheffield the train would detach its two restaurant cars and three other carriages before heading west to Penistone and then north to Huddersfield for a 10.20 p.m. arrival in Bradford. The train quickly became popular and the Eastern Region transferred a number of Gresley A3 Pacifics to Leicester shed in 1949 to work the heavy train (loading twelve or more carriages) over the Leicester-London section. By 1956 it appears that the Low Moor Cl.5 now worked the Up train to Leicester, where the A3's took over, and returned with the Down train in the evening. From 2nd January 1960 this train ceased to run any more because all such express services on the old Great Central route were discontinued in the first tentative moves by the London Midland Region (who had taken over in 1958) to close the GC route completely.

Shortly after leaving Bulwell Common, the Annesley DIDO makes its way northward hauled by N7 No.69651. In Great Central and early LNER days the motive power used on the DIDO was usually a locomotive dedicated for the purpose and Annesley shed would have a least two engines available for the turn. Then, the engines were drawn mainly from classes which had seen better days or were working out their remaining years on traffic which was in no way 'taxing' with only two or sometimes only one bogie coaches making up the train, but it was nevertheless important enough to demand a reliable locomotive. In British Railways days the same criteria applied concerning reliability but any locomotive 'on shed' could have been drawn upon for the job. So, it was not unusual to see the likes of a Thompson B1 working the DIDO one day and then an N7 the next. Of course the tank engines were preferred but in the event of a failure anything would do. No.69651 came to Annesley in December 1951 from Colwick shed where it had arrived during the previous April. The N7 stayed at Annesley until September 1956 when it returned to the former Great Eastern area working from Cambridge shed. For the DIDO job it was fitted with push-pull gear and had its Westinghouse brake replaced by a steam brake. Besides No.69651, three other push & pull N7's joined the Annesley stud: No.69691 from 4th November 1951 to 30th May 1954; No.69695 from 4th November 1951 to 16th May 1954, and No.69692 which had three separate but short 'residencies' - 16th May to 17th October 1954; 14th November 1954 to 6th February 1955 and 13th February 1955 to 30th September 1956.

After the N7's had returned south it was left to one of the old-timers to run the DIDO as here in January 1956 with C12 No.67363 working the service at Bulwell Common after a fall of snow. The Atlantic tank was allocated to Annesley shed from February 1949 to 14th October 1956 when it went to Tilbury of all places. During its seven year stint at Annesley, for which it was specially push & pull fitted, the C12 had a three month visit to Stratford shed. C12's were no strangers to Annesley shed as six of them had been allocated to the depot during various periods in the LNER era. However, only two of the class joined the shed during the BR period - No.67363 as here and 67387 from 13th November 1949 to 23rd December 1951.

Bulwell viaduct, 30th August 1955, with Thompson B1 No.61155 of Doncaster heading a six-coach northbound working whilst an express approaches from the north with V2 No.60890 in charge. In the foreground is the Great Northern Leen Valley line curving eastwards towards Bestwood. Below the viaduct the Midland's own line through the valley of the River Leen passes beneath along with the aforementioned river and two main roads. The three rail routes which dominated this valley vied with each other for the lucrative coal traffic generated by the large mines situated along its length. The Midland, being here first, had the easiest of the routes and, for a couple of decades at least, very little competition. The Great Northern chose a steeply graded route but with little in the way of major engineering works. The Great Central, being the last to arrive had to take a more difficult route hence this viaduct, however, their gradients were less severe than those of the GN route. Alas, less than seventy years after building possibly the best railway route in the United Kingdom, the Great Central's main line to London was closed. Bulwell viaduct was demolished in 1981.

To cater for the weekend and evening needs of the Nottingham 16A based engine which worked the branch line through Southwell, the Midland Railway built a small shed at that place but in January 1955 it closed and responsibility for working the branch passed to the nearby ex-Great Northern engine shed at Newark. which was, at that time, a sub-shed to Retford. The motive power employed on the branch consisted, in its latter years, a pair of Johnson 0-4-4 tank engines fitted for push-pull working. In 1957 Nos.58065 and 58085 had the job and the former engine is seen on arrival at Rolleston Junction with its single carriage. The Eastern Region shedplate adorning No.58065 had just been fitted in exchange of the 33A Plaistow shedplate from where the 0-4-4T had previously been allocated, actually working from Upminster shed. The first station at Rolleston Junction was opened in July 1847 and was apparently named Southwell Junction. It closed and re-opened twice more before finally becoming fully operational as Rolleston Junction in September 1860. This establishment is still open but the passenger service on the branch to Southwell finished in June 1959.

Out on the old Great Central at New Basford in September 1956, the former Great Northern J6 0-6-0's were still working plenty of passenger trains. Although looking the worse for wear, No.64249 climbs away from New Basford station with a service to Derby at 8 p.m. on Thursday 6th. Note the trap point guarding the Down main.

Basford (North) circa January 1954 with Colwick based J6 No.64257 entering the station with a Derby (Friargate) to Nottingham (Victoria) stopping train. The coaching stock is an interesting mixture with the rear three vehicles appearing to be Brake Seconds. Looking at the passengers awaiting the train, it is difficult to realise, some fifty-odd years on, that most of them will have passed-on by now. The two young ladies on the right of the picture, if still with us, will now be drawing their old age pensions. For a Colwick engine the J6 is looking remarkably clean but perhaps the fact that the engine had just completed a 'General' overhaul at Doncaster works a few weeks previously might have some bearing on its appearance. A relative newcomer to the Colwick fold, No.64257 was transferred to the Nottingham depot in February 1951 in a move which was to prove to be its last before withdrawal in June 1960.

23

Another long-time Colwick resident was J5 No.65490, seen here at DAYBROOK FOR ARNOLD whilst working a Nottingham (Victoria) - Basford (North) local loop line service in 1952. The 0-6-0 had another year of employment in front of it before withdrawal on 11th October 1954 and its external condition would not get any better than this. Built in October 1909 as Great Northern Railway No.31, it became LNER No.3031 on 10th March 1925 being renumbered at Retford shed, its home at that time. In September of that year it transferred to New England but was back at Retford six months later. Its move to Colwick took place in July 1938 and at that time Colwick housed fifteen of the class with the other five resident at Retford. During its forty-five year life, No.65490 had eight different boilers each one staying with the engine for about five years, on average, although boiler No.1375, which was put on in August 1914, was with the engine until September 1923. As can be seen, the station was still gas-lit at this time and would remain so until its premature closure in 1960. When first opened this station was named Bestwood & Arnold but before the first year of services were finished it was renamed Daybrook for Arnold & Bestwood Park. Later in 1876 it became just Daybrook. However, as we can see from the nameboard it changed once again to a double-barrelled title.

Daybrook, Saturday 2nd April 1960, just before disaster hit this important route. Known locally as the 'Back line' the ex Great Northern line from Colwick, through Gedling and Basford out into Derbyshire and beyond, was known as the Derbyshire Extension and was built to enable the GNR to access the lucrative coalfields of Nottinghamshire and Derbyshire. The huge marshalling yard at Colwick was created to sort the large number of coal trains which used this route daily. Coal was the life blood of the GNR but they still put on facilities for passengers as per this station at Daybrook in the northern suburbs of Nottingham. When this line was opened in 1875 passengers wishing to reach central Nottingham from here had to board an eastbound train and travel a circuitous route via Mapperley tunnel, Gedling, and then Colwick where their train headed west towards London Road station. Even when the GN's Nottingham suburban railway was opened in 1889 the journey was not much shorter with three intermediate stations and some ruling gradients. With the coming of the Great Central, who created their new station Victoria in the centre of the city by tunnelling through the sandstone below Carrington, the GNR were able to cut their Basford-Nottingham centre journey times by nearly a half, the Derby trains also benefited by this new, faster route out of the city which connected to the old route at Bagthorpe junction. However, the GN still ran a portion of their passenger services over the old route and those were perpetuated into BR times as here with K3 No.61974 on the 1-28 p.m. Basford (North) to Nottingham (Victoria) via Gedling calling at Daybrook with its three coach load. photograph - D.H.Beecroft.   25

No.61974 gets its train underway and starts to tackle the short rise to Arno Vale with the lightweight load. Note the London Midland Region non-corridor suburban coaches making up the train - well I suppose this line and indeed the railways of Nottingham were by then part of the LM Region. The K3 is in remarkable external condition for a Colwick engine although it had been into Doncaster works during the previous February but only for a Non-Classified repair. It left Colwick for Immingham at the end of the year and managed to eke out a living until July 1962.

WD 'Austerity' No.90389 confidently wheels another load of coal over the 'Back line' through Daybrook, towards Colwick yard in April 1960. Colwick shed had probably the largest allocation of these uncomfortable but sturdy and hard working 2-8-0s. BR scrapped all 733 of them.

Hauling a fitted freight westbound through Daybrook that Saturday was Colwick K3 No.61833. After the gruelling climb from Colwick yard through Gedling and Mapperley tunnel, the crew were given some respite by Arno Vale and were now keeping the train in check over the downhill gradient all the way to Basford. Daybrook had quite extensive goods facilities but by 1960 these had fallen mainly into disuse as if by premonition of what was to occur in the not too distant future. In the left background is the Be-Ro flour mill, a one-time household name which of late is never seen. The station here closed on Monday 4th April 1960 because of the collapse within Mapperley tunnel - the 'Back line' was no more. photograph - D.H.Beecroft.

Robinson O4 No.63657 climbs towards Arno Vale and eventually Colwick yards in the time honoured tradition of hauling Nottinghamshire coal out of the Leen Valley to send south and east where no coal exists. It is Saturday 2nd April 1960, spring is well on the way, the sun is shining and traffic is moving - for now. The 2-8-0 was possibly the last of its kind to pass through Mapperley tunnel with a loaded mineral train because after the engineers take possession of the tunnel on Saturday night it will never re-open. The 'Back line' would become a backwater and everything west of Mapperley ridge would close. The tunnel collapse was a stroke of luck for the railway authorities because they wanted to run-down Colwick yard anyway and then transfer all the traffic to Toton yard - the LMR was in charge by now. So, just to throw a spanner into the conspiracy works, was the tunnel sabotaged to speed up the run-down? It was the sixties and funny things were happening on the railway, what with Dr Beeching, dieselisation, etc.... Just beyond the bridge spanning the A60 Mansfield Road, was the junction for the erstwhile Nottingham Suburban railway which closed to passengers in July 1916. After it was singled in February 1930, the lines stations and yards closed to goods traffic in the following January but through goods trains used the line until May 1941 when the Luftwaffe brought an end to those by bombing and severely damaging the embankments at the southern end of the line near Trent junction. However access to the branch from the north was still possible to certain commercial concerns along its length but these eventually could not be viably operated and the line finally became defunct. The last section of track and the connection to the main line here at Daybrook junction was lifted in February 1957. Note the two coal wagons in view, a five plank 10 tonner and the, by now, ubiquitous 16-ton mineral wagon. Their contents appear to be excellent examples of the locally mined hard black stuff. photograph - D.H.Beecroft.

Colwick motive power depot mechanical coaling plant in May 1955 with O4 Part 8 No.63628 topping up its tender. This 2-8-0 was a recent convert to the Part 8 division within the O4 class, its previous identity had been as a Part 5 engine when a shortened version of the O2 type boiler was fitted. It now had the 100A (B1) boiler, side window cab, all mod cons! and would continue to work for BR for another ten years but not from Colwick shed as it transferred to Mexborough in January 1956. The mechanical coaling plant was built as part of the modernisation of Colwick motive power depot and became operational shortly before the outbreak of war in 1939. It was equipped with two 250 ton capacity bunkers and became a landmark from miles around. photograph - D.H.Beecroft.

Tucked away at the side of Colwick shed in June 1955 with a pair of J52 was this N5, No.69286. Built in September 1894 by Beyer, Peacock for the Manchester, Sheffield & Lincolnshire Railway this old lady was working until withdrawn from Langwith Junction depot in November 1960. As LNER No.5748, it first came to Colwick from Barnsley shed in December 1930 (it was one of three new 0-6-2T sent to Barnsley in September 1894) but moved on to Annesley in March 1932. Ten years later it was allocated to Derby Friargate shed which was a sub of Colwick and it continued in residence there until June 1948 when it returned to Annesley. A four year spell at Woodford Halse started in December 1949 and from there it started a second stint at Colwick in November 1953. At the end of 1955 it moved on to Darnall and whilst there it was given a General overhaul during the summer of 1957. Still in relatively good condition it transferred to Langwith in April 1959 to begin its last posting. photograph - D.H.Beecroft.

Coming off the line from Trowell junction and joining the Leen valley line at Radford junction on 4th November 1955, Kentish Town 'Jubilee' No.45557 NEW BRUNSWICK brings a London bound express into Nottingham from Leeds. Delivered to Crewe North in July 1934 by the North British Locomotive Co., as unnamed No.5557, the engine was attached to a 4,000 gallon tender No.9004 but in about 1936, when it was named, it swapped that tender for a 3,500 gallon tender (No.3918) which had been with a 'Royal Scot'. It kept that tender throughout its life, as here, and was scrapped with it in December 1964. NEW BRUNSWICK spent its first four years on the Western Division at both Camden and Crewe North but in July 1938 it took a permanent transfer to the Midland Division, and went to Kentish Town. Just after the outbreak of war it went to Bristol Barrow Road shed for the duration of the conflict. Derby shed was the next recipient in July 1946 but later the following year it returned to Kentish Town for a twelve year residence. Derby got it back in November 1959 and held onto it for exactly two years before relinquishing it to Burton. Two and a half years at Burton hauling anything meant that the end was not too far away and a move back to Derby in June 1964 sealed its fate and it was condemned in September. It went for scrap to Cashmores at Great

Bridge in December.

In this undated British Railways period view of Radford station and its junction, Westhouses based 3F 0-6-0 No.43825 drags a mixed freight across the junction from Trowell and the Erewash Valley main line. Straight ahead is the Leen Valley line which generated a lot of coal trains through this station up until the end of mining in the valley. Passenger services from Worksop via the so-called Robin Hood line still use this route whilst the line to Trowell is also busy with cross-country passenger services from the north-west to the eastern counties. Radford station was opened by the Midland Railway in 1876, re-sited from an earlier 1848-built station situated nearby. This station closed on 12th October 1964 and was demolished. In this late summer evening picture the place looks fairly tidy but the lack of passengers, intending or otherwise, is a clue to its demise under the Beeching axe. The Deeley 3F moved to Westhouses shed in July 1956 from Toton and was withdrawn in April 1962 so that helps us pin down the date to a six year period within that time frame. photograph - D.B.Swale.

33

Lenton South junction, January 1955 with Fairburn 2-6-4T No.42174 heading out of Nottingham towards Derby with a stopping passenger train. We have already met this engine at Beeston on Christmas Eve 1955 so we will have a look around the junction here on this somewhat grotty day. The lines going off to the left go to Mansfield via Lenton North junction and Radford. The four tracks forging straight ahead comprise two passenger lines on the left with the other two being designated as good lines. On the far right is the branch line to Clifton Colliery.

Approaching Lenton South junction, Ivatt Cl.4 No.43018 has charge of a midday Leicester (Midland) - Nottingham (Midland) stopping train circa July 1953. This view looking westward towards Beeston and Trent highlights some of the signalling controlling this junction and the junction for the Clifton Colliery branch going off to the left. The 2-6-0 had been a resident of Nottingham Midland shed from new in June 1948 until July 1952 when it transferred to Leicester Midland shed. No.43019 was another which came new to 16A in June 1948. Four more of the class also came to the depot new from their makers: 43033 May 1949 to June 1957; 43040 July 1949 to April 1958; 43118 June 1951 to October 1952 and 43119 July 1951 to October 1955. No others ever came and none of these six ever returned to Nottingham. The last statement is not strictly true where No.43018 is concerned. It did arrive new in June 1948 but after a week it went on loan to Colwick then, later in the month it was sent to Ardsley of all places for a period of loan, returning to Nottingham Midland in August but the loans did not constitute a permanent transfer so, in essence the statement does stand up.

Just near the junctions at Lenton was Nottingham Midland motive power depot - 16A. The date is 27th May 1957. We have a new locomotive, old buildings. The 9F, No.92131 has just come into traffic from Crewe works. Although initially allocated to Saltley, the engine went instead to Toton and is probably the reason why it is visiting Nottingham; none of the class were ever allocated. Still so new you could smell the paint, the 9F was to have a short life with just ten years in front of it when this photograph was taken. It did not yet have a cast iron shed plate fitted to the smokebox door. To the right of the 2-10-0 is the derelict Outdoor Machinery Department building with the hydraulic accumulator house standing erect and tall, whilst beyond that, and towering above nearly everything, is the mechanical coaling plant. Behind the tender is the No.3 shed which came into operation in 1893 and had the biggest turntable of the three roundhouses at 60ft diameter; Nos.1 and 2 sheds each had 55ft examples.

Just one year earlier, 27th May 1956, these two 350 h.p. diesel-electric 0-6-0 shunters, 13246 and 13247, had arrived at Nottingham, new from Derby works and in green livery. These were not the first of their kind sent here, as four other Derby built machines had arrived in October and November 1954. Like most steam sheds which had some of these diesel shunters allocated, Nottingham struggled to maintain a 'clean area' for their everyday care. However, this class of diesels were not ones for hanging about their home depots anyway and tended to spend most of their lives actually working, sometimes around the clock, not going near the shed except to refuel and to check the oil and water levels. They were hardy machines and a tribute to their designer. Towards the closure of Nottingham engine shed in April 1965, a number of Type 2 Bo-Bo diesels came but their number were few; Toton was not too far away and they had enough diesel locomotives for everyone. Both these engines were eventually renumbered with the D prefix, D3246 in December 1960, D3247 during the following March. D3246 ended up at Bletchley being withdrawn in May 1982 as 08178. The other went to work from Crewe diesel depot but was condemned in June 1975 as 08179. Both ended up at Swindon works for scrapping.

Newton Heath sent this Stanier Cl.5, No.44845, to Nottingham in February 1958 with an excursion from Manchester and in this afternoon view on 16A shed the 4-6-0 is coaled up, turned, watered, labelled and ready to work back home with C889. Just what the working entailed and why, is unknown to the writer. This Cl.5 was a virtual native of Manchester after starting its career in November 1944 at Belle Vue shed. After twelve years there it had to move over to Newton Heath because its own depot was closing down in April 1956. It then spent another twelve years at Newton Heath prior to being withdrawn in the summer of 1968. photograph - D.H.Beecroft.

Too big to enter No.3 roundhouse to stable, Trafford Park 'Britannia' No.70004 WILLIAM SHAKESPEARE is put to bed in the sunshine at Nottingham Midland shed in August 1959. The Pacific had worked in from Manchester (Central) on an unknown duty but it is not yet turned and ready to head home, although the content of the tender appears to have been taken care of. This engine had spent its formative years, from September 1951 to June 1958, working from Stewarts Lane shed on the Southern Region hauling named trains such as the GOLDEN ARROW, and NIGHT FERRY, but it was not confined to the South Eastern Division of that region and would often work South Western Division trains to Southampton and Bournemouth. Its great moment of glory occurred in 1951 when it was exhibited at the Festival of Britain in London. Although allocated to Stratford shed when new, it never got there and was instead sent straight to the South Bank site then, when the festival was concluded, to Stewarts Lane shed to earn its keep. Its appearance now is hardly to exhibition standard but what else could one expect from Trafford Park shed where cleaning locomotives was not at the top of their agenda. photograph - D.H.Beecroft.

'Royal Scot' No.46112 SHERWOOD FORRESTER, complete with badge, inside No.3 shed at Nottingham in April 1960. This 7P had transferred to 16A from Leeds Holbeck during the previous December, its first ever tenure to Nottingham although it was a regular visitor when working the Leeds-London expresses. Although it was never allocated to a Nottinghamshire depot until now, the 4-6-0 was to spend its last years working from this depot and later, from September 1962, nearby Annesley. At some point during its time at Nottingham Midland the nameplates were removed, no doubt for safe keeping, and never put back on. Even the steel backing plates to which the nameplates were attached were also taken off. Note the different designs of smoke trough in this shed. photograph - D.H.Beecroft.

Back on the main line and slightly back in time to May 1956, the afternoon of Sunday 27th to be exact. Traffic, like all Sunday working over British Railways, was quiet and a good time to visit engine sheds. Passing Nottingham Midland shed that afternoon, with a stopping train for Leicester, was one of the Leicester Midland's BR Standard Class 2's, No.78029, which had arrived new at 15C from Darlington works in July 1954. In the right background, just behind the signal, is the lofty seven storey grain warehouse built by the Midland Railway amidst their sprawling goods yard and warehouses which dominated the north side of the main line west of Midland station. Now nothing of that large facility survives, the main goods office, where my father worked is now a magistrates court. Although the day was sunny and fine for photography, it was not unknown for flood waters to inundate by a couple of feet, the area within the picture.

Saturday 12th March 1955 - Nottingham.

Association Football has always been a passionate game, no matter at what level or class of football a team may be playing. Virtually every town and city in Britain has a football team representing it in one of the major leagues. Some places have two or more 'local' teams and passions tend to run higher in those particular towns especially when a 'derby' game is played - the following at these venues is almost tribal. One of the oldest and most popular domestic knock-out competitions which takes place every 'season' is the FA Cup competition when even non-league teams can take part and with an element of luck can reach the latter stages of the ties. On Saturday 12th March 1955 Notts. County had been drawn against York City with a home advantage which meant that York supporters had to travel to Nottingham by what was then the usual mode of travel over long distances - by train. That day no less than twelve specials were run, eleven from York and one from Scarborough, for the York City supporters and the accompanying table lists the arrival times and to which Nottingham station the trains ran into. Also listed is the motive power and from which shed it came from. In an effort to try and capture all the visiting engines on film, I literally ran between London Road High Level and the Midland station but alas I did not get all of them. Note that ten Thompson B1's arrived along with two V2's and the engines I missed on camera - the V2's. For the record, the crowd at Notts. County that day was just over 47,000, the biggest attendance in the team's history. However, York City won the game and went on to the semi-final - probably one of their more glorious periods.

Below are listed the trains with the motive power used. For the record, those engines using Midland station went to Midland shed for servicing whilst those on the London Road trains went to Annesley.

Arrival Time	Station	Locomotive	Shed
10.52 am	London Rd.	61289	Darlington.
11.04 am	London Rd.	60917	Doncaster.
11.06 am	London Rd.	61017 BUSHBUCK	Neville Hill.
11.16 am	London Rd.	60949	Gateshead.
11.26 am	Midland	61086	Neville Hill.
11.40 am	Midland	61060	Dairycoates.
11.55 am	Midland	61068	Botanic Gardens.
12.22 pm*	Midland	61074	Dairycoates.
12.50 pm	London Rd.	61338	York.
1.00 pm	Midland	61016 INYALA	York.
1.11 pm	London Rd.	61224	York.
1.23 pm	London Rd.	61015 DUIKER	York.
1.29 pm	Midland	61304	Botanic Gardens.
1.36 pm	London Rd.	61038 BLACKTAIL	York.

* from Scarborough.

Besides the eight Notts. County-York City game excursions, Nottingham Victoria handled thirty-eight separate extra trains that Saturday. Many were passing through, en route to Wembley for the Women's Hockey International at the Empire Stadium, and had originated at Doncaster, Sheffield, Retford, Mansfield and even Derby, besides a couple starting from Victoria. In a northerly direction five more football specials passed through carrying Wycombe Wanderers fans to an amatuer cup-tie at Bishop Auckland.

My first picture of the procession of football specials, albeit a distant shot of B1 No.61017 BUSHBUCK at London Road High Level. Thankfully the sun was superb, intense even, on this basically winter Saturday but my own excursions between the two arrival stations became intense also. Luckily for me the authorities decided not to use Victoria as a receiving station, or so I thought. A number of trains from Yorkshire and other places did in fact work into and through Victoria from the north but these had nothing to do with the Notts County game nor even football so their continuous procession on the GC bridge over Midland station was simply a sidetrack to me.　　　43

Having already missed No.61086, another rare Neville Hill B1, at Midland station, I did manage to catch No.61060, one of the Dairycoates
44 engines which turned up that day. This and the other B1 visitors to the Midland station went off to 16A for servicing and stabling.

Fifteen minutes later an immaculate No.61068, of Hull Botanic Gardens, arrived at Midland's platform 1. The B1 had completed a general overhaul at Doncaster works just a few weeks previously so that probably accounts for its smart turn out.

As soon as No.61068 had moved off to the carriage sidings, the third Hull based B1, No.61074 of Dairycoates shed, appeared with excursion No.905 from Scarborough. The train stopped in the same spot alongside ex Midland 2P No.40411, the Nottingham (Midland) station pilot for the day.

Not wishing to leave out a long-time Nottingham resident, I 'bagged' the 2P on station pilot duty on that excellent Saturday in March 1955. In fact the 4-4-0 had only been at 16A since the previous September but it was to become a firm favourite for this duty for a number of years afterwards.

The next football excursion arrived at High Level station but I missed getting a photograph of it. I nevertheless made my way back there hoping for further arrivals. During my short transit a named B1 came into Midland and I was unfortunate not to get that on film too but at least I copped it, however, persistence with the camera paid off and I got this nice shot of No.61224 entering from the east - the first York engine of the day on film. The municipal gasworks forms a nice industrial townscape background.

Another 'namer' but alas not a cop. Exactly twelve minutes after the arrival of 61224, Thompson B1 No.61015 DUIKER came into High Level having travelled the same route as 61224, via the ECML, Newark, Bottesford North and West junctions, and Trent Lane junction. The station staff did wonders that day getting the trains emptied of, admittedly eager, passengers and putting up with spotters, photographers and normal passengers - but then that was normal for the period when many more people travelled by train to football matches and other sports venues.

My last and probably favourite shot of the day's visitors. B1 No.61038 BLACKTAIL arrived at High Level just a few minutes after 61015 had departed. This York based 4-6-0 stopped in the right position for the light. The driver has just changed the lamps for an empty stock movement and will depart for Bagthorpe (Basford North) carriage sidings once the signal is given. Built on a brick arched and steel girder viaduct, with an arm of the Nottingham canal on the north side and the municipal gas works on the south side, the somewhat hemmed-in London Road High Level station was opened in March 1899. With the reduction in status of the Victoria station into an unstaffed halt on 3rd July 1967, High Level station closed. The station nameboard, just visible to the left of the platform lamp standards, proclaimed not just the station name - London Road Nottingham - but also a legend inviting cricket and football fans to alight there for the Trent Bridge grounds. I wonder who managed to salvage that wonderful piece of social history?

On the route of the football specials from the ECML to London Road High Level was Radcliffe-on-Trent. The station was opened in July 1850 and the eventual facilities included a goods yard with shed, coal siding, weighbridge for road vehicles, a waiting room on the Up platform, and full station facilities within the Down platform buildings. A new signal box, opened in 1874, replaced an earlier cabin and was provided for the opening of the GN&LNW Joint line junction at Saxondale some two miles to the east. In 1891 the line between Radcliffe (as the station was known up to 1871) was quadrupled as far as Saxondale junction by the inclusion of a set of goods or slow lines. In the summer of 1954, J6 No.64238 starts to climb the 1 in 132 gradient as it accelerates away from the station with an Up stopping train to Grantham from Nottingham (Victoria). The stock is a mixture of Gresley and Thompson non-corridor coaches which worked on this service until the coming of the diesel multiple units in the latter part of the decade. In 1968 the station became an unstaffed halt and its buildings were demolished in 1971. In 1974 the station name reverted to Radcliffe and inadequate lightweight shelters became the only passenger accommodation. The signal box was replaced by a ground frame in November 1963 but the goods yard remained open for another eight months afterwards.

Grantham based J6 No.64237 comes out of Victoria Street tunnel and negotiates the curve onto the former Great Northern metals at Weekday Cross junction in 1950 with a Derby (Friargate) -Grantham stopping train. At this point the engine is still on a ruling grade of 1 in 193 up to London Road High Level station after which it will ease before falling to Trent Lane junction. The 0-6-0 had started its LNER career working at Colwick shed but in October 1933 it transferred to New England. Grantham got the engine in May 1946 and this working is typical of the work it did from that shed. In February 1953 No.64237 moved south to Hitchin, its last allocation before withdrawal in November 1959. The BRITISH RAILWAYS lettering on the tender was applied at a 'General' repair carried out at Doncaster works in November 1948, and was the identification used prior to the introduction of the BR 'lion & wheel' emblem. The BR lettering adorned this engine's tender until January 1952 when the J6 again visited Doncaster works for overhaul.

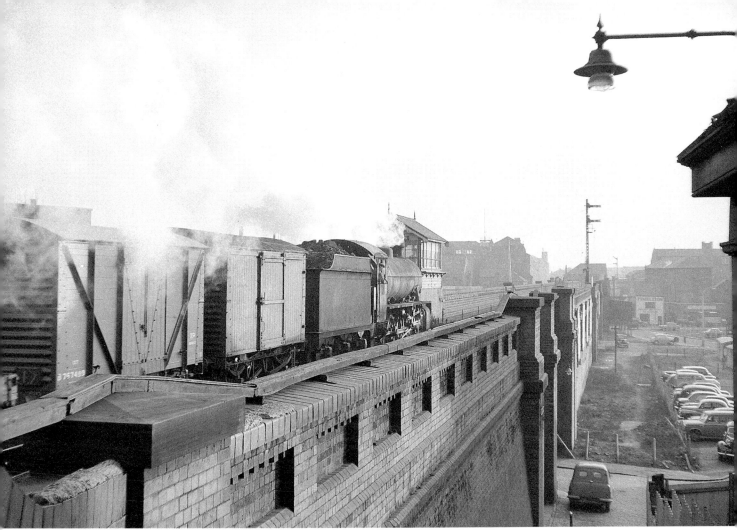

After taking some photographs at Midland station on Wednesday 28th December 1955, I took the short walk to Weekday Cross junction and in the low weak sunlight managed to capture Thompson O1 No.63578 as it galloped across the viaduct with an Up fitted freight. This Annesley based 2-8-0 was one of the twenty-five O4 rebuilds which were carried out at Gorton in 1945. Superb performers on the Annesley 'Runners' to Woodford yard, their reign was somewhat shortened by the arrival of the BR Standard 9F 2-10-0 and, when the London Midland Region boundaries took in Annesley shed and the ex Great Central route, a mass withdrawal of the O1's was carried out and perfectly good locomotives, some only recently back from overhaul at Gorton, were consigned to scrap. This particular engine went to Derby works for cutting up as did many other Annesley O1's and, what Derby did not take care of Crewe works scrapped. This once interesting and busy piece of railway infrastructure in the centre of Nottingham was threatened with total extinction when the GC line closed. The bridge over Midland station was taken down, Victoria station was demolished to make way for the shopping centre but a very short section of this viaduct managed to resist so that today it forms part of a new concrete viaduct on which stands the last station, and temporary terminus, of the Nottingham tramway system. Hopefully the tramway will one day extend over the Midland station on a new bridge and then over the Trent to take in the southern suburbs of the city on new routes and trackage. Whatever happens, this morsel of the GCR is still with us for many years to come. So, next time you're over this part of the city use a little bit of imagination and try to visualise scenes like this - its amazing what comes past.

A side view of the same stretch of viaduct as seen from Broad Marsh before another shopping emporium was built. Crossing the viaduct with a northbound freight is Annesley based Thompson O1 No.63650. Now this engine, another of the 1945 rebuilds, was more fortunate than many of its kin which stayed at Annesley because in February 1957 it transferred to March shed in Cambridgeshire, then in February 1960 it went to the former GCR shed at Staveley to enjoy another five years of work in the coalfields under the protection of the Eastern Region. Its final move was to Langwith Junction shed on 13th June 1965 but it was condemned a fortnight later. Ironically it returned to East Anglia a few months later but this time as scrap destined for R.A.King's yard in Norwich.

When the Manchester Sheffield & Lincolnshire Railway extended their main line to London at the end of the nineteenth century, they had to expend vast amounts of money in the Nottingham area. Whereas the northern approach to the city was via a series of high embankments and then tunnels, the southern section consisted a tunnel, long viaducts and a number of girder bridges. This spectacular four track bridge crossed the River Trent just to the west of the city centre and is a mixture of cast iron and steel. The three girder spans were each 112ft long. The two lines on the east side of the bridge consisted the main line whilst those on the west side served Queen's Walk goods yard. Note the seven arch brick built viaduct linking the bridge to the southern embankment. This short viaduct spanned the southern flood plain and was substantially built to withstand the surging flood waters which occasionally encroach on the shore. Normally, an embankment would have been constructed to the river bank but because Clifton Colliery was situated on the north bank just to the west of the bridge, flood waters could not be allowed to build up west of this bridge in case they inundated the underground workings of the mine. Behind the camera, on the north bank of the Trent, the MS&LR had built a large goods yard (Queen's Walk) complete with a warehouse, suitable cranage, an eight road carriage shed and a four road engine shed, the latter hardly used for the purpose, especially after Grouping. The Darnall based Thompson B1 is No.61316 heading south with a Sheffield to Leicester train on 11th April 1955.

I apologise if the next two pictures appear not to adhere strictly to the remit as described by the title of this album. The pictures might be set in Wales but they do concern Nottingham and the people thereof. Read on. In its bid to win back passenger traffic from alternative modes of transport, British Railways introduced, in vast numbers, the diesel multiple unit trains from the mid-1950's. As each area got, or was about to get, these new, clean, comfortable, fast, efficient trains, the authorities would usually organise a day trip to somewhere nice at enticingly low fares using the new, revolutionary transport. On Sunday 1st June 1958 it was time for the Nottingham Division to show-off their latest trains in the form of these Birmingham Railway Carriage & Wagon built d.m.u's. The destination for the day-trip, which incidentally was sold out - Bettws-y-coed in North Wales. The first picture shows us excited, happy and gay passengers making their way along the platform towards the exit. The driver leaning out of his cab window to observe the throng is obviously proud of his new train

and the fact that so far the whole experience has gone well.

This illustration shows the nine car train (3x3-car units) taking up the whole platform. Already the tail lamp has been placed and once the driver has settled himself at the opposite end of the train, it will set off to Llandudno Junction to be stabled for the afternoon. My reason for including these two views, besides the Nottingham connection - they show BR trying its best; people are actually socialising and happy; personnel were proud of the job they did; the sun always shone during those post-war summers.

Nottingham (Victoria) 7th August 1956. J6 No.64248 heads a Grantham stopping service at bay platform 11 and alongside at bay platform 12, a B1, hiding its identity with a rush of steam, is in charge of an all stations service to Leicester. The J6 class was by now getting 'a bit long in the tooth' but nevertheless were still the mainstay of local services on the former LNER lines around Nottingham. A relative newcomer to Colwick shed, No.64248 had arrived during the previous November from Boston shed where it had worked for most of its life except for an eight year stint at New England which commenced in December 1932. During it last six months at the Peterborough depot it worked on the former Midland & Great Northern Joint line. Built at Doncaster in January 1918, it was condemned there on 4th March 1959 and later scrapped. Over on the engine servicing line in Parliament Street dock, another B1 prepares for a southbound working.

Woodford Halse allocated BR Standard Class 4 No.76035, draws away from its train at Victoria station after a midday arrival on 3rd March 1956. This train might have been one of the important cross-country services brought to Nottingham by the Cl.4 after failure of the original train engine. Only three years old, the 2-6-0 appears decidedly filthy but we can at least spot one of the visual detail differences which set this engine apart from earlier members of the class. Built at Doncaster in 1954, No.76035 was the first of the class fitted with plain rather than fluted coupling rods. On delivery this engine went to Neasden shed but ten months later it transferred to Hitchin from where it worked semi-fasts into King's Cross and from there to Cambridge but that work was short lived and Woodford got it in June 1955. That depot used it on semi-fast passenger services from Leicester to Marylebone amongst other duties. Four months after this photograph was captured No.76035 moved back to Neasden and managed a residency of six years there prior to moving across London to nearby Cricklewood. Whilst at Neasden it would work freight to Woodford but went further afield with semi-fast passenger services to the likes of Leicester. It was even observed in Yorkshire during June 1960 heading a Scarborough bound holiday extra. It certainly got as far as York and may well have carried on to Scarborough assuming its six tons of coal was enough. In December 1964 it moved to another London depot - Willesden but its work still included running on the old GC route out of Marylebone. After seven months at Willesden it migrated northward with the rest of the steam population and ended up at the former LNWR depot at Chester where, in May 1966, it was withdrawn.

It was not everyday that Gresley A4's ran into Nottingham (Victoria), or indeed any other station in Nottingham for that matter. However, on 12th May 1956, A4 No.60014 SILVER LINK, the first 'Streak' built, and on this day still attached to one of the original corridor tenders (No.5590), brought an Ian Allan excursion, complete with some Pullman coaches, en route from London to Manchester, through the station. Immaculately turned-out by King's Cross shed, No.60014 had also recently finished a 'General' overhaul. I can still hear that chime whistle now. Withdrawn 29th December 1962, the Pacific entered Doncaster works for the last time on 16th January 1963 and was broken up.

The stairways leading to Parliament Street at the southern end of Nottingham (Victoria) offered a fine vantage point from which to photograph the train movements at the station. In the mid 1950's J6 No.64215, which spent most of its LNER life and all of its British Railways existence working from Colwick shed, has just started off from the middle siding between the Down fast (platform 4) and the Up fast (platform 7) with the empty stock for a afternoon local working to Grantham. Platform 7 has a large number of passengers waiting to board this train when it sets back into the platform. The bay platforms 11 and 12 already have stock in them to form local workings to Basford & Bulwell via Netherfield, and another to Newark. In the right background an unidentified Thompson B1 comes off the turntable ready to take up a southbound working.

Just after midday on a Saturday in early March 1949, Annesley based J11 No.64318 gets the signal to depart platform 3 at Nottingham (Victoria) with a stopping train to Mansfield. Except for an eleven day loan to Ardsley shed in August 1935, this J11 had been allocated to Annesley since 30th June 1933 having previously been shedded at Immingham. In this view the 0-6-0 is looking fairly clean but that is because it had recently returned from overhaul at Gorton works when it was renumbered from 4318 and its tender was lettered with the wording BRITISH RAILWAYS. Extremely reliable engines, most of the J11's could be called upon for mixed traffic duties but they excelled in moving goods trains. Numbered 1011 by the Great Central then 6011 by the LNER, No.64318 was built by Neilson Reid in May 1902 and worked for just over sixty years before being condemned at Gorton works in August 1962.